FILTON
TO
SEVERN BEACH
IN OLD PHOTOGRAPHS

FILTON
TO
SEVERN BEACH
IN OLD PHOTOGRAPHS

COLLECTED BY
JOHN HUDSON

ALAN SUTTON
1988

Alan Sutton Publishing Limited
Brunswick Road · Gloucester

First published 1988

Copyright © 1988 John Hudson

British Library Cataloguing in Publication Data

Filton to Severn Beach in old photographs.
1. Avon, history
I. Hudson, John
942.3'9

ISBN 0-86299-463-2

Typesetting and origination by
Alan Sutton Publishing Limited.
Printed in Great Britain by
WBC Print Limited

CONTENTS

INTRODUCTION 6

1. HIGH DAYS AND HOLIDAYS 9

2. FILTON 19

3. PATCHWAY 43

4. STOKE GIFFORD 49

5. FILTON AT WAR 55

6. ALMONDSBURY 65

7. VILLAGE LIFE: OLVESTON, TOCKINGTON AND LITTLETON-ON-SEVERN 87

8. THE PLANEMAKERS 103

9. CHARLTON: THE LOST VILLAGE 119

10. AUST, THE FERRY AND THE SEVERN BRIDGE 127

11. NEW PASSAGE AND SEVERN BEACH 139

ACKNOWLEDGEMENTS 160

INTRODUCTION

Long before local government reorganisation in 1974, the corner of south-west Gloucestershire that fringed the North Bristol suburbs owed more to the great city to the south than to the county town way up along the A38. Not all of it had itself been suburbanised – indeed, by no means all of it is suburbanised to this day – but Bristol was the only logical focal point for major shopping sprees, pantomimes and music halls, and trains for the annual week at the seaside.

It was inevitable that, when the city began to expand in the 1920s and '30s, this was one direction in which it would grow, and only the Second World War has put a temporary brake on the relentless growth since then. Through the 1960s the emphasis was on housing and, while the estates still burgeon round Patchway and Stoke Gifford, warehousing, high-technology industry and out-of-town shopping are becoming ever more prominent at Cribbs Causeway, Aztec West and other sites fringing the M4/M5 interchange.

Such moves were probably an unavoidable consequence of having one of England's most famous road junctions and a major river crossing on one's doorstep, though it is interesting to recall the motorway planners' early insistence that their aim was simply to speed travel between existing communities, and not spawn housing and industrial developments at every access point. Perhaps the surprise is that this dream survived for as long as it did.

For someone with roots two hundred miles north of here, I have strong folk memories of Filton and Severn Beach, stretching back for as long as I recall. My father's Uncle Horace moved south to Filton in the 1920s, and every summer a big brown cardboard box of greengages from his garden would arrive on our doorstep in Lancashire. Dad would tell us tales of his orchard in the sunny, sheltered Severn Vale, of his collection of Chelsea china and of walks across fields on balmy Sunday evenings to the Salutation pub beside the old church at Henbury. Nobody in our family had made it big in remotely the way Uncle Horace had, and that land of plenty known as Filton was very much a part of the myth.

Dad would sound only one word of warning, based on his visits some twenty or thirty years earlier, in around 1930. 'There's a very funny place down there called Severn Beach,' he would say. 'They go there in their thousands down there, and I can't think why.' Years later, when I moved to this area in 1976, he could offer me only one piece of advice: 'There's a very funny place down there called Severn Beach. Don't live there.'

Of course, I had to visit it to find out why, and it was a sad sight, with the Blue Lagoon in ruins on the seafront. It was only comparatively recently that I began to discover the old press pictures and postcards of the little resort in its heyday, with hordes of trippers thronging its dubious beach and shanty town of attractions. This was the Severn Beach that my father knew, the one on which he had based his judgement. Today it is all very different, even from my first experience of it a dozen years ago, trying only to be a community serving its growing number of residents, and succeeding rather well so far as one can tell.

My father visited Uncle Horace while on marathon cycle rides from the North, and I followed in his tread-marks in 1962, crossing the ferry to Aust and pedalling up the road to Almondsbury past late-summer orchards heavy with fruit. By then the mythical uncle had long since departed his earthly paradise of Filton, but memories of those greengage summers flooded back, and I thought of them again when studying that wonderful photograph of potato-growers that forms the cover of this book. It is marvellous growing country around here, even though the major cash crop in Filton and Patchway these sixty years past has been semi-detached and bungalows.

Most of the pictures in this volume span the years between 1880 and 1960, with perhaps a greater emphasis than is usual in this series on the 1920s, '30s and '40s. I am particularly grateful that the area includes such unique features as the Severn Bridge and, indeed, Enoch Williams's ferry that preceded it; the aircraft factory; the lost community of Charlton; and yes, even that 'miles-of-smiles' Severn Beach of the 1920s and '30s. Needless to say, I am equally grateful to the contributors who helped me cover these phenomena in some little depth.

As I note on page 120, there is perhaps a tendency in some people's minds to exaggerate the size of Charlton, the community swept aside for runway extensions in preparation for the ill-fated Brabazon at Filton in the late 1940s. British Aerospace remain slightly sensitive about the issue to this day, to the extent that their public affairs people disagree with my description of it as 'a lost village'. But the fact remains that 'Charleton' appears on Saxton's map of Gloucestershire of 1577, but is nowhere to be seen on the current Ordnance Survey sheet 172, and the camera surely does not lie when it shows a settlement with a green, a pub, a post office, a little tin church and houses ranging from ancient cottages to substantial farms.

A few words about my choice of photographs. I have tried hard for human interest, my great rule of thumb being a conscious effort to avoid good 1885 views that look like bad 1985 ones. The captions are as informative as space, initial information and the success of further research will allow, and I hope the facts and figures are as accurate as I believe them to be; as for my opinions and speculations, you may take them with as large a pinch of salt as you feel they warrant.

Acknowledgements for the loan of pictures and information can be found on page 160, and I am grateful for the great kindness, help and co-operation I encountered almost every step of the way. I hope I offend no contributor if I make mention here of the especial support and encouragement of Mr W. Leslie Harris, Mr Colin Powney, Mrs Betty Rickards, Mr Michael J. Tozer, Miss Mary Trevelyan and Mrs Valerie Vizard. And I think my dear recently-departed father and his Uncle Horace were somewhere out there too, shrugging their shoulders in disbelief as I watched the sun set over Newport from a peaceful and civilised Severn Beach.

John Hudson,
Gloucestershire, 1988.

SECTION ONE

High Days
and
Holidays

THE CROWNING OF THE SEVERN BEACH CARNIVAL QUEEN, early 1930s, with a sea of happy faces and some fine examples of the fashions of the day. Performing the ceremony is Bob Stride, the moving force behind Severn Beach's phenomenal popularity as a day trip destination in the 1920s and '30s. A section on the resort and its older neighbour, New Passage, begins on page 139.

MAY DAY, Knole Park, 1914, and the stewardesses gather round the maypole before going out among the crowds with sweets and refreshments. The home of the Chester-Masters was a focal point of Almondsbury life on the big patriotic days, and older residents still find it hard to believe that only its fifteenth-century tower now survives. A section on Almondsbury and its people begins on page 65.

VICTORY PARADE, Filton, 1945, with troops filing past the saluting platform on the corner of Braemar Avenue. The sun is shining brightly and the crowds are out in force, but this was still a time for military precision rather than a spontaneous outpouring of joy. A section on Filton at war begins on page 55.

THE PLOUGH INN, Filton in 1912, when Philip Shield of the prominent local family was licensee. The regulars are obviously up to something here — I take them all to be men, the voluminous skirts notwithstanding — but the fact that Raffles is on the Ground means nothing to even the keenest local historians today. For more of the day-to-day life of Filton past, see page 19.

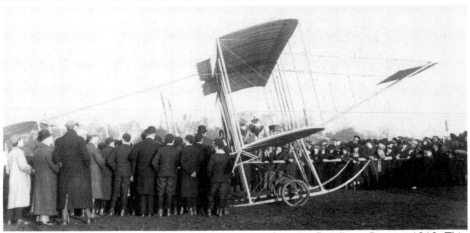

SIR GEORGE WHITE'S FILTON-MADE BRISTOL BOXKITE on show on Durdham Downs, 1910. This self-made millionaire first came into contact with the infant aviation industry a few years earlier, when as chairman of Imperial Tramways and a newly-created baronet, he began taking holidays in the South of France. Within a year of this eyecatching stunt his British and Colonial Aircraft Company had won an export order for eight Boxkites to the Tsar's Russia, and the First World War clinched the company's success, while hastening the demise of its founder through over-work. A section on Filton's fascinating aviation history begins on page 103.

A WELCOMING PARTY stands beneath a triumphal arch at the entrance of Almondsbury's Knole Park estate to greet Major Richard Chester-Master on his return from the Boer War in July 1901. The sequel to the story was not so happy. The major, by then a lieutenant-colonel, died in the First World War in 1917, and it was this that prompted his widow to sell the Knole Park estate three years later.

A FRIENDLY SOCIETY gathers on Whit Monday 1903 at the Beaufort Arms, Stoke Gifford, complete with band and banner. Publican Joe Powell is on the right, in shirt sleeves and broad-brimmed white hat. A section on Stoke Gifford begins on page 49.

TRIUMPHAL ARCH at the entrance of Tockington Village. The lender of the picture surmises that the date is 1918, but 1901 and the end of the Boer War seems at least as likely. For more on Tockington and the South Berkeley Vale villages, see page 87.

ALMONDSBURY PLAYERS' PANTOMIMICS TROUPE in 1948, looking less than inscrutably oriental in Aladdin.

ROYAL SEAL OF APPROVAL. The Queen inspects work on Concorde in British Aerospace's Brabazon hangar at Filton in September 1966.

THE SEVERN BRIDGE was officially opened by the Queen, accompanied by Prince Philip, on 8 September, 1966. The picture shows Her Majesty on the Aust observation platform after the ceremony with the Minister of Transport, Mrs Barbara Castle. A section on the bridge and the earlier ferry begins on page 127.

A HIGHSPOT of the Queen's silver jubilee visit to Bristol on 8 August, 1977. Some 30,000 people, mainly children, turned out to welcome Her Majesty at Filton High School playing fields – among them two-year-old Andrew Ford of Rockhampton, near Thornbury, whose shy presentation of a bunch of red, white and blue sweet peas from his parents' garden set hundreds of cameras clicking.

SECTION TWO

Filton

FILTON HILL in the early 1900s. The rectory entrance is on the extreme right, while on the left is Fairlawne House, home of the aircraft and tramways magnate Sir George White. The gabled house beyond the horse-drawn cart is Rodney Hill Farm.

Valentine Leaving Bristol, Daily Mail Race

JUST TWO YEARS AFTER SIR GEORGE'S BOXKITE MADE ITS SENSATIONAL DEBUT on Durdham Downs, this far more sophisticated looking monoplane attracted a mixed group of interested onlookers as the air ace Valentine piloted it from the grounds of Conygre House, Filton, in the Daily Mail round-Britain race of 1912.

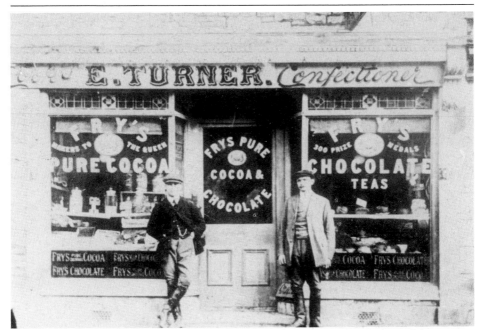

EDWARD TURNER'S CONFECTIONERY SHOP, Filton Hill, *c.* 1910, in a row on the site of the present Jet garage. His daughter Freda Turner, seen here outside the shop, was a familiar sight around Filton in the 1930s with her Walls Stop-Me-And-Buy-One pedal tricycle. Tubs were 4*d*., choc ices 3*d*. and Snofrute lollies 1*d*.

EDWARD TURNER'S BREAD VAN, C. 1919. A hand cart for shorter local deliveries was also part of his fleet.

FYLTON STORES, next to Turner's, in around 1900. The property was later occupied by a branch of Bristol Old Bank – latterly the National Provincial – before demolition. The stores, run by R. Parsons, sold everything from groceries to hardware – all 'At City Prices', for better or worse.

THE CONGREGATION at the Methodist Chapel, Church Road, a scene of stark simplicity relieved only by the oil lamp and the lady's splendid hat.

FILTON BAND in Wades Farm orchard, 1908 – with flat caps outnumbering trilbies by twelve to four.

ST PETER'S PARISH CHURCH before 1905. The man above is looking over the wall into the Cotthay, an ancient enclosure that became part of the churchyard in that year. The picture below shows the creeper-clad church shortly after the Cotthay, in the foreground, had been added to its grounds. The church looks ancient, and indeed it dates from the fourteenth century, but it was rebuilt almost entirely in 1845.

The Church Filton.

TWO CLERICS who served Filton parish church for more than seventy years: above, James Bedford Poulden was curate from 1829 to 1831 and rector from 1831 to 1876 while his successor John Mackie, right, served until 1902. He was succeeded in turn by his son John Henry Mackie, who stayed until 1915, and their contribution to the community is marked in the street name Mackie Road.

A CRUCIFER leads the Bishop of Bristol and the rector, the Revd C.R. Haslum, at the consecration of the parish church extension on 25 March, 1961. This major work, introducing a new nave, sanctuary and spire, realigned the church and made it almost unrecognisable from the earlier photographs.

THE OPENING OF THE WAR MEMORIAL HALL crowned years of enthusiastic fund-raising in 1927, but by 1962 it was gone, the victim of road-widening. A similar community effort during the 1960s resulted in its replacement, the Folk Centre at Elm Park, in 1967.

A MARVELLOUSLY ATMOSPHERIC VIEW of the church and Church Road, c. 1950, with men walking and cycling to work on a bright winter's morning. On the left is the gable end of the old village school, while a sign on the church hut announces that this is the site of the enlarged parish church, still a decade away at the time.

THE TRAM TERMINUS showing left, the tram into Bristol, and right, the bus to Thornbury, plus a fair cross-section of the road traffic of the First World War era – a hand cart, a motorcycle combination and a horse-drawn milk wagon. Evans' grocery is on the right, while the sign on the side of the building advertises W.S. May, the Stoke's Croft tailors.

LOOKING NORTH TOWARDS THE TRAM TERMINUS at much the same time. Filton Laundry is advertised on the vehicle, while the hoardings on the cottages on the corner of Church Road have signs for such old favourites as Bovril, Topical Times and Camp Coffee.

FILTON in 1946, a picture that evokes the austerity of the post-war years. On the right are the cottages between the Plough and Horseshoe, then the Hillcrest Cafe, later the White House and now long gone. The trees on the left stood in front of the old village school.

LOOKING NORTH TOWARDS CHURCH ROAD in 1935, at the height of the inter-war building boom. The large sign to the right of the church advertises Ideal Semi-Detached Homes from £350. And on the right of the picture, Northville Building Co. advertises houses and bungalows at Filton, Patchway and eight other sites from £350 to £700 – all at 14s. per week, including rates, plus 'a reasonable deposit'.

A SIMILAR SCENE in the 1950s, reminding us that pedestrian crossings with stripes were not with us until several years after the end of the war.

THE HORSESHOE INN in 1881, an ancient thatched property demolished entirely to make way for the present building.

LOOKING NORTH from the corner of Church Road towards the terrace housing Turner's confectionery and the Bristol Old Bank on Filton Hill. This was before the height of the great building boom of the 1930s; Northville Building Co.'s homes begin at £400 or £1 a week, and that was far beyond most people's pockets. The hoardings sing the praises of Wye Valley Strawberry Jam – The Jam in the Diamond Jar – Ashton Gate Beer and greyhound racing at Knowle.

THE COFFEE SHOP, opposite the Anchor Hotel, on the site of what is now Filton Technical College's Shield House. Dinners and teas were advertised as they still are in chip shops in the North of England, making it clear that dinner comes before tea.

A CHARA TRIP leaving the Coffee Shop, 1920s.

A 'CASTLE' CLASS LOCO hauling *The Bristolian* at Filton Junction in the 1950s. Both the engine and the station are no more.

JOHN AND ELIZABETH COLLINS. John farmed Wades Farm from 1858 to 1909.

SAMUEL SHIELD, founder of Filton Laundry, with his suitably well-pressed wife and seven children, c. 1890.

FILTON LAUNDRY'S HORSE-DRAWN FLEET, c. 1906. Beyond the main block is the Laundry House, now occupied by Lloyds Bank.

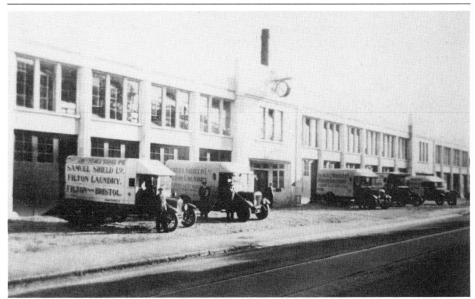

FILTON LAUNDRY TRUCKS, C. 1923. After the First World War the carriage works closed, and its buildings were taken over by the laundry. When the laundry, in turn, ceased trading in 1951, the block was used by Bristol Cars and Bristol Siddeley Engineering until 1965. It is now Filton Technical College's Shield House, recalling the name of the Laundry's founder.

FILTON LAUNDRY FOLDERS of the 1920s.

A WORLD OF BROWN PAPER, string and wicker skips – packers at Filton Laundry in the 1920s.

WHEELWRIGHTS at Robert Phillips's works, with examples of their craft. Phillips's Coach and Carriage Works, opened in the 1880s, was next to Filton Laundry.

FILTON HOUSE c. 1900. Built as a farmhouse in 1720, it was taken over by Sir George White as his aircraft company HQ in 1910, and is now the British Aerospace headquarters at Filton. The people in the picture are possibly Edwin Shellard and his family, after whom Shellard Road is named.

INSPECTOR, is he . . . dead? A 1930s Filton Amateur Players' production in the War Memorial Hall.

TRAFFIC PROBLEMS, 1922-style. Spectators leave Filton Aerodrome after competitors in the round-Britain race had flown for Croydon.

BELLE VUE, 'the Red House', in Conygre Road, the home of Samuel Shield, c. 1890.

PUPILS OF FILTON SCHOOL, 1910, with their headmaster William Nation Baker, staff and older scholars. Children were presented with a medal after each year's regular attendance.

CHILDREN OF SHIELD ROAD SCHOOL, September 1961, with a novelty harvest loaf baked by John Williams of Cheltenham Road, Bristol.

FILTON CARNIVAL STEWARDESSES selling sweets to raise funds to build the War Memorial Hall, which opened in 1927. The stall on the right sold nothing but cigarettes and tobacco.

LADY WHITE opens the Sea Cadet Corps' Filton unit, the Training Ship *Endurance*. This particular land-locked ship was later scuppered to make way for Northville Post Office.

THE ANCHOR HOTEL C. 1910. The notice on the front of the building advertises the Bristol Festival production of *Elijah*, while the large sign on the side wall tells of tea gardens, parties catered for 'on the shortest notice', good stabling – a point on which publican Pope prided himself – and accommodation for motorists and cyclists.

THE ANCHOR POND C. 1903, with the Anchor Hotel on the left and the Coffee House on the right. Perhaps entirely coincidentally, a deep puddle is still prone to form on the road at the roundabout that now occupies the site.

FILTON PARK AND THE CABOT CINEMA, 1935. It is obviously a busy shopping day, but the young woman with the push-chair is hardly taking her life into her hands as she crosses the road.

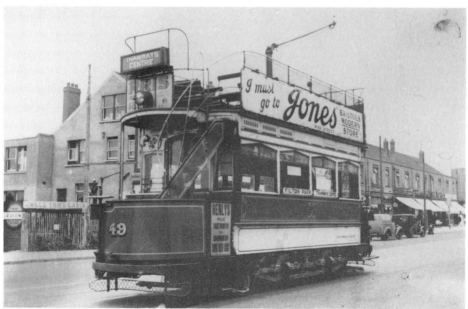

TRAM NO. 49 AT FILTON PARK, 1930s. On the left is Uncle Tom's Cabin, a popular meeting place in the inter-war years.

SECTION THREE

Patchway

THE ALMONDSBURY–PATCHWAY–FILTON BUS, 1900 – with four outside, six inside and luggage space aplenty.

STATIONMASTER MOORE AND HIS STAFF at a quiet Patchway Station in 1912.

THE FIRST BUS FROM FILTON TO THORNBURY crosses the railway bridge at Patchway in February, 1906. Within weeks the open-top deck was abandoned after passengers had complained of danger from overhanging branches.

THE CRICKETER IAN BOTHAM, a silly hat and no end of well-wishers make their steady progress through Patchway during his fund-raising walk to Land's End from John O'Groats in November, 1985. Leukaemia victim Nicola Buxton, aged ten, has just presented him with a cheque for £1,300 on behalf of Downend Junior School.

TWO NOT ALTOGETHER INVITING VIEWS of the Railway Hotel in the 1920s, a building now earning its keep as a car showroom. The tea gardens were popular with cyclists and families with young children.

PATCHWAY SCHOOLS in 1930. The two groups of children in the yard were practising a sword dance.

THE NEW INN, 1923, a small pub at the top of Patchway Common.

A PATCHWAY SCHOOL TEA PARTY at The Grange, Woodlands Lane, Almondsbury, the home of Mrs D. Smith.

Stoke Gifford

THE CHURCH AND VICARAGE, STOKE GIFFORD.   No. 363.

THE VICARAGE AND ST MICHAEL'S CHURCH, Stoke Gifford, in around 1906. The church dates from medieval times and its churchyard still has an old-time rural air, in spite of encroaching housing and the roar of trains through Bristol Parkway station just yards away.

THE BEAUFORT ARMS, C. 1910, showing several superficial changes from the Whit Monday scene of 1903 on page 14. Today the logo of a restaurant chain dominates the building, and only the eagle-eyed can be aware that it remains the Beaufort Arms.

THE GREEN, STOKE GIFFORD.

The 'Progress' Series, No. 360
Printed in England. I.H.S. & Co., B and C

STOKE GIFFORD has changed beyond all recognition in the years since the war – except around the Green, where much would be instantly recognisable to our great-grandfathers. The picture above, c. 1908, shows the post office building before it was extended to the left and the school with an unfamiliar porch above the man's head. Below: from a slightly different angle and progressing into the early 1920s, we see the newly-extended post office row, the school minus the porch and the recently dedicated war memorial. The school was closed in July, 1988, with children moving to far larger premises in Meade Park.

A CHARMING LITTLE GROUP OF PHOTOGRAPHS showing a family growing up at Stoke Gifford Post Office in the years before the First World War. At the top of the facing page we see Mr and Mrs Taylor in 1896, with their daughter Sylvia the little dot sitting by the gate. Below: the scene moves on to 1905, by which time Sylvia has been joined by Kathleen and Jessie. Above: the years have ticked by to 1915, the little dot of 1896 stands imposingly at the fence in front of the doorway, and a smart young chap in a boater seems to have found his way into the picture too. Mr Taylor was postmaster at Stoke Gifford from 1893 to 1935.

ROCK LANE, Stoke Gifford, 1908. The Baptist Chapel on the left was completed in the previous year.

STANLEY FARM, now sadly derelict, was one of many handsome buildings sold by the Beaufort estate when it disposed of its Stoke Gifford holdings in 1915.

Filton at War

GRIM FACES in 1914 as men of the Sixth Gloucestershire Reserve march down Station Road, Filton to an uncertain fate.

THE DEDICATION OF FILTON WAR MEMORIAL, August 1920, a moving ceremony for the still recently bereaved.

GEORGE VI AND QUEEN ELIZABETH inspect a Beaufort with Mr C.F. Uwins at the Filton works in February 1940.

MRS CLARICE DAVIES AND A FRIEND survey the wreckage of her bombed house in Filton Avenue, August 1940.

QUEEN MARY, resident at Badminton for much of the war, visits the decontamination and rescue centre at Braemar Avenue with Mr St Leger Yeend, clerk to Sodbury Rural District Council. The building later housed the branch library.

ANOTHER BOMBED HOUSE IN FILTON, 1941. The Anderson shelter in the garden saved the family's life.

THIS UNEXPLODED BOMB lay undetected for many months in Boverton Road, Filton Avenue, before being removed in April 1941.

TWO DRAMATIC SCENES from a Civil Defence/Air Raid Precautions exercise in the grounds of Conygre House in 1942.

QUEEN MARY watches Filton Civil Defence members go through their paces in an exercise at Badminton in 1943.

HMS FILTON was the WVS's eye-catching contribution to the Warship Week parade of 1942, seen here at the top of Southmead Road.

SAILORS MARCH PAST THE SALUTING PLATFORM in the Warship Week parade of 1942. On the right a number of little boys do their best to get in on the act. Below, the part that women played in the war effort was a prominent feature of Salute the Soldier Week, 1944.

CHEERFUL MEMBERS of the Filton Home Food Production Society's co-operative potato scheme epitomise the Dig for Victory spirit in this superb picture from 1944. There was always a strong interest in keeping allotments and smallholdings in the country north of Bristol, and the large number of able-bodied men who stayed at home on essential work in the aircraft factories ensured that the tradition was more than upheld during the war.

THE POTATO CO-OPERATIVE still hard at it in 1946. A pillbox stands between their fields and the trees lining Golf Lane.

MARY, DUCHESS OF BEAUFORT, accompanied by Mr H.J. Hunt, passes a guard of honour to unveil the Second World War memorial in the War Memorial Hall in June 1948. When the tablet was later moved to the Folk Centre in September 1967, the Duchess was again on hand to perform the ceremony.

Almondsbury

THE GRACE FAMILY CRICKET TEAM at Knole Park, c. 1867. W.G. is the youthful figure on the left while Dr E.M., known as The Coroner, is centre in the middle row. Father, Dr H.M., is the imposing figure in the stovepipe hat – but as cricketing lore has it that it was his wife who taught the boys to play, it is a pity that she is not in the picture too.

FILTON PRIZE BAND leads a group of First World War veterans down Over Lane to the war memorial cross on the Horseshoe Bend, c. 1928. The cross was financed by the family of Colonel Richard Chester-Master, the Boer War hero who died in the Great War in 1917.

ALMONDSBURY CRICKET CLUB'S EASTER MONDAY OUTING to Cheddar, April 1928. The lender of this photograph, Miss Mary Trevelyan, is the small white blob peeping over the side of the charabanc.

MR FRED BRACEY at his home 15 The Village – now in Townsend Lane – in 1935. An elderly retiree, he came with his wife Annie to live in Almondsbury with his daughter, Mrs Maud Trevelyan.

FINE HATS AND FUR COLLARS. An expectant audience at the Parish Hall, Gloucester Road in 1928.

THE OLD HILL STORES, 1910. Across the Gloucester Road from the present one, it was demolished in 1964 when the motorways came to Almondsbury. John Wesley is said to have stayed at the cottage next to the shop.

THE OLD POST OFFICE on the Gloucester Road. A hairdresser's shop now occupies the nearer building, with Rocklands Restaurant beyond.

PEACE PAGEANT, Oaklands, 1919, with members of the armed forces marching past St George and Britannia.

A RATHER LESS SOLEMN CELEBRATION OF VE DAY, 1945, with the officer and sarge playing cards in their cushy billet. The signs epitomise wartime humour: 'If you know a better 'ole, go to it!'; and 'Hotel Ritz, Bread and Breakfast, Manager Hammonde Deggs'.

THE OLD SWAN, Gloucester Road, 1910. The sign tells of good stabling, but the car speaks of a new age of travel.

ALMONDSBURY HILL AND HILL HOUSE, 1910. Road widening has taken its toll on the triangle of green at the top of Over Lane.

MUSIC HATH CHARMS. Almondsbury Women's Institute toy band, 1929.

THE QUARRY on the scarp immediately below the Gloucester Road. Since the local building tradition favours rendered walls, many Vale communities had quarries producing rubble stone sufficient for most everyday needs. In recent times, with the fashion for stripping rendering, hundreds have discovered to their cost that the protective covering was there for a very good reason.

THE GREEN ON ALMONDSBURY HILL, 1910, looking north up the Gloucester Road towards the hospital, then less than twenty years old.

SEVERN VIEW TEA ROOMS, 1920s, one of any number of such establishments which served cyclists and motorists on and around Gloucester Road north of Bristol.

SUNDAY SCHOOL OUTING to Severn Beach, 1944. Following an old tradition, the children travelled on carts lent by farmer Edgar Keel of Court Farm, though the big lads prided themselves on blazing the trail on their bikes. The lower picture shows farmer Keel with Canon and Mrs Charles Mayall.

THE BERKELEY HUNT meets on the Green, Lower Almondsbury in 1947.

ANOTHER GLIMPSE OF THE BERKELEY HUNT MEET at Lower Almondsbury, 1947. In the background on the right is the huge pink marble obelisk that dominated the view of the church from this angle before permission was gained to have it removed.

ELDERLY FACES and some strikingly young looking ones: Almondsbury Observer Corps at the height of the Second World War. The proximity of Bristol, Avonmouth Docks and the Filton aircraft works made theirs no easy task.

YOU MOVE AND I'LL MURDER YOU ... Four little boys do their stuff for the photographer, 1917.

NURSES AT THE HOSPITAL, 1920. Built in local Cattybrook brick, with stone dressings, it was opened by the Duchess of Rutland in November, 1892. The architect was C.E. Ponting, who was also responsible for the fine oak reredos in St Mary's Parish Church.

ALL GIRLS TOGETHER. Above: Almondsbury Girl Guides chose a dull day for their trip to Weston while camping at Woodspring Priory in 1922. It was sunny for the spud-bashers below in 1929, however, when the camp was at Sapperton in the Cotswolds.

TWO FINE ALMONDSBURY HOUSES still doing good service. Above: Woodhouse, which remains in private hands, and Oaklands, now an old people's home. Woodhouse was the home of Dr Basil Harwood, who was ninety when he died in 1949. He is still remembered locally as a Norfolk jacket-clad figure on a bicycle – and internationally as the writer of hymn tunes named after churches at which he played the organ. 'Thornbury' is probably the best-known.

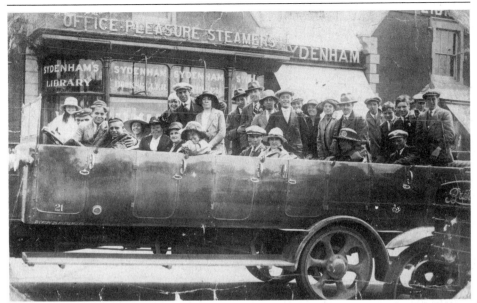

THE OAKLANDS STAFF OUTINGS of 1922 and 1923, the latter to Weymouth. The house was owned from 1891 by Mr Hiatt Baker, a prominent Bristol businessman and another keen cyclist. He would pedal to Patchway station to catch the train into town.

THE VIEW OVER LOWER ALMONDSBURY from the hill in the years before post-war building expanded its boundaries.

ST MARY'S CHURCH in the 1920s. It is a prominent landmark in the Vale, with its thirteenth-century tower surmounted by a fine lead broach-spire.

ONE DAY BILL PARKER RAN OUT OF WATER AT MEREBROOK FARM, out on the Tockington road. He drove his cart up to the village pump at Lower Almondsbury, a cameraman was on hand, and the result was perhaps the best-loved of all old pictures of the village.

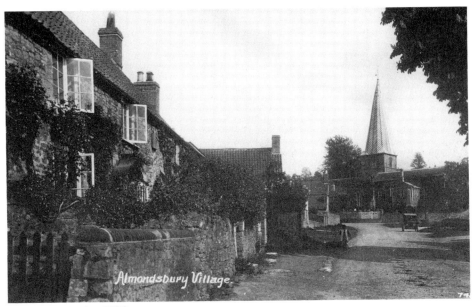

THE VILLAGE in the 1920s.

THE TWO GREAT LOST HOUSES OF ALMONDSBURY. Above: Knole Park, and below: Over Court. Knole Park was a Tudor mansion built by Thomas Chester, mayor of Bristol, and sold to a speculative builder by his descendants in the inter-war years. A modern house now adjoins its sole remains, the fifteenth-century tower. Over Court, another Elizabethan pile, was once famous locally for its deer park – and White Lady ghost. It stood empty from the 1940s, and was eventually demolished in 1981 after a fire four years earlier had left it in a perilous state. Modern houses now occupy the site, but the fine eighteenth-century clock tower remains.

OVER COURT.

CATTYBROOK BRICKWORKS, C. 1923. Third from the left on the front row is Mr Bill Hulbert, the works manager. Bricks are still made at Cattybrook, Ibstock Building Products having taken over the plant in 1972.

THE ARCHITECT MR R.E. SLATER got a large brush, painted an X on the countryside east of Almondsbury, and said: 'We'll have the M4/M5 junction right there...' That, at least, is how it seems in this remarkable picture from the early 1960s, with the lines of the converging motorways being carved out of the landscape. In the foreground is the A38 at the northern end of the village, with Hortham Hospital mid-way up the picture on the left.

Village Life Olveston, Tockington and Littleton-on-Severn

ABOVE: YOUNGER PUPILS OF OLVESTON SCHOOL, pre-1910, and below: a less-than-action shot of a group going home a few years later. One postcard manufacturer was convinced that the village was Oliveston.

OUT OF SCHOOL, OLIVESTON.

OLVESTON UNITED in the early 1930s, just a few years after their formation. The lads still play in yellow and blue, the regimental colours of Colonel Turner of Old Down, an early benefactor. Second from the right on the front row is Mr 'Lord' Stovold, father of the Gloucestershire cricketer Andy and his former county colleague Martin.

VOLUNTEERS FROM OLVESTON and Tockington made up the Sixth Gloucestershire Battalion E Company's 52 Platoon in the Second World War.

POST OFFICE, OLVESTON.

TWO VIEWS OF OLVESTON VILLAGE, c. 1910. The old post office, above, is now Sedgeley, the house next to the Methodist Church. Signs advertise Brooks the dyers in Bristol and the Bristol Times and Mirror.

WALTER E. DOBLE & Co.

CHILDREN AROUND THE WAR MEMORIAL beside St Mary's Church, Olveston, c. 1920. The large pinnacles atop the Norman tower were added in 1606, after the church had been damaged by lightning.

OLVESTON VILLAGE in the 1920s. The shop on the left is the present-day post office.

THE EARLY TUDOR GATEHOUSE of Olveston Court Farm, happily still intact. The farm was a manor of the Denys family, huge landowners in the countryside around Bristol.

MR H.A. LEAKEY'S BREAD VAN outside his shop in Tockington, at the side of what is now the recently-restored house known as Two Ways. The pony is held by the baker's son.

LEAKEY'S SHOP is to the left of the black-clad lady in this view of Tockington from c. 1910. The house on the left can be seen in the picture of the triumphal arch on page 15.

TOCKINGTON VILLAGE

A LATER PICTURE OF TWO WAYS, Tockington, c. 1950, with the George's house the Swan Inn on the right. By this time Leakey's shop had been taken over by the miller and corn merchant George Dawes.

A VIEW FROM THE LAST CENTURY of the cottage No.3, Tockington Green, with the Methodist Chapel to the left. Signs of decay are already apparent in the tree that dominated the Green for so many years. Odd fact: the cottage has now shed its porch – and the chapel has gained one.

ABOVE, THE BEAUFORT HUNT'S BOXING DAY MEET on Tockington Green, c. 1905, and below, the Green from a similar angle in the 1920s, with Mustay House on the right. The wall that surrounded the tree remains, the bed now planted with flowers and a sapling.

SIMILAR VIEWS OF TOCKINGTON GREEN from the Olveston road, the tree again dominating the picture.

TOCKINGTON is a favourite spot among judges in Avon's best-kept villages contest. Here Sir John Wills, right, presents the 1978 Armstrong Cup for small villages to Mrs Muriel Vowles, chairman of Olveston Parish Council.

HOME FARM, Littleton-on-Severn, with a group of people including Mrs Joseph Taylor and her five children. The house is now the home of Mr John Taylor, son of the tallest boy in the group on the left.

LADS FROM LITTLETON fishing in the Severn mud for 'flatties', c. 1922.

MOSES WHITE, skipper of the Littleton Pill sailing barge *Matilda*, c. 1918.

LITTLETON PILL drew in crowds from miles around in January 1885 when a huge whale was stranded in its narrow waters. Some 68 feet long, it pulled in 40,000 onlookers in a fortnight before it was towed away to Avonmouth to be converted to fish manure. The area of the pill is known as Whale Wharf to this day.

MOSES WHITE'S *MATILDA* in the pill below the brickworks, c. 1920. Built in 1830 and now buried beneath the mud of the pill, she plied the Bristol Channel ports carrying bricks, coal and sand.

RESIDENTS OF BRICK COTTAGES, Littleton-on-Severn, outside their homes c. 1910. The terrace was built by George Wintle to house labourers at his Littleton Brickworks; families down that way tended to be large, with the result that the cottages were more often known as Bunny Row.

MISS EATON AND HER CHARGES at Littleton School. c. 1905.

PATRIOTIC CELEBRATIONS AT LITTLETON, almost certainly to celebrate victory at the end of the First World War. In the top picture, which shows the procession coming up the lane from the rectory, a torn poster advertises a sale at Lodge Farm by the auctioneers Luce, Young and Alpass.

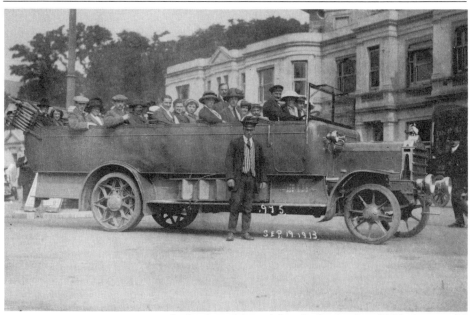

VILLAGE OUTINGS FROM LITTLETON. In the top picture, taken in September 1913, those solid tyres took the trippers all the way to Bournemouth.

The Planemakers

THE FATHER OF THE FILTON AVIATION INDUSTRY, Sir George White, who founded the British and Colonial Aircraft Company in 1910. It became the Bristol Aeroplane Company in 1919, three years after his death, and is now part of the British Aerospace conglomerate.

SIR GEORGE'S FILTON WORKS in 1911, after his successful publicity for the Boxkite aircraft had brought in orders from several sources, including the Tsar of Russia. Like so much else at the factory in those days, the production of propellers was a job for skilled woodworkers.

TWO MORE VIEWS OF THE WORKS in January 1911, with work progressing on Boxkites and other experimental aircraft.

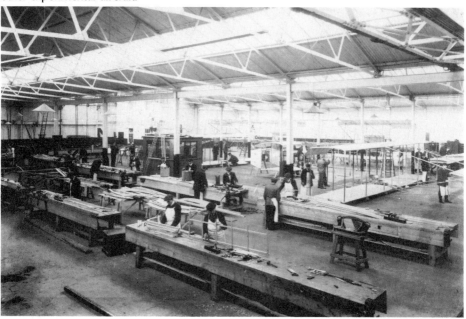

AEROPLANE PARTS FOR EXPORT in 1920. The crates on the front truck are bound for the Chilean airforce at Valparaiso.

THE AIRCRAFT ORDER BOOK was not always so full in the early years of the Bristol Aeroplane Co. This is the scene in February 1921, when a shortage of work saw motor body-building introduced, on Armstrong Siddeley and Bristol Tramways bus chassis.

CYCLING TO WORK at the aircraft factory, c. 1930. On the left is Evans' Grocery in Filton, while Rose Cottage, now demolished, was on the site between the Plough and the Horseshoe.

THE BRISTOL AEROPLANE CO'S SUCCESSFUL CRICKET TEAM of 1926.

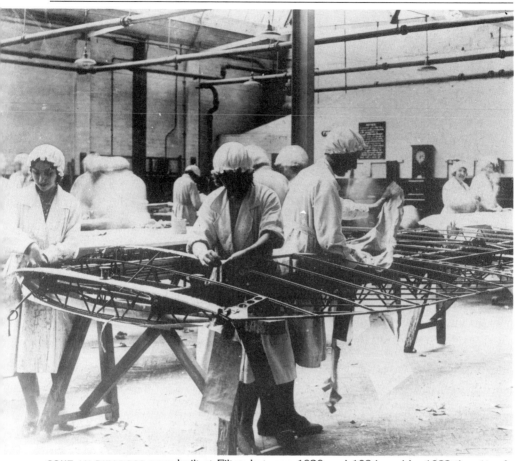

SOME 441 BULLDOGS were built at Filton between 1929 and 1934, and by 1932 the aircraft was equipping ten of the RAF's 13 fighter squadrons. This picture shows women at work on the canvas wings of an early model.

THE BULLDOG PRODUCTION LINE in the early 1930s. The aircraft was first conceived as a private venture by Leslie Frise in 1926, and the first flight, by Cyril Uwins, came in May 1927. By 1936 it was in use by nine national air forces.

A SUPERB AERIAL VIEW of the Bristol Flying School in 1934, with the first signs of housing development on the road beyond.

HIGH NOSTALGIA. A Bulldog pays a sentimental return visit to Filton in 1961. At the bottom left of the picture is the newly completed church extension, while prefabs line the playing field side of Shellard Road.

THE FACE OF THE FUTURE? BAC employees inspect the first Brabazon in its specially constructed hangar in July 1949.

A SHAPE THAT ONLY BRIEFLY MADE ITS MARK ON THE SKIES. The Brabazon takes off on speed trials in October 1949.

BRAVE SMILES. The Brabazon test pilot Bill Pegg, left, with company VIPs.

THE MOTORCYCLIST'S HEAD TURNS as the first Britannia produced for BOAC undergoes trials. The handover took place in December 1955. Below, lunchtime workers flock around the company's demonstration aircraft on her return from a flag-flying visit to the United States in August 1956.

THE BUSY SCENE IN THE BRABAZON HANGAR in July 1957, with Britannias destined for BOAC and El Al nearing completion.

A PICTURE THAT CAPTURES SOME OF THE EXCITEMENT OF THE EARLY CONCORDE YEARS. 002, the second prototype, nears completion, while beyond it work progresses on the first sections of the airframe for 01, the first pre-production model.

THE FINAL THREE CONCORDES to leave Filton, nose-to-tail in the Brabazon hangar in August 1979.

Charlton: The Lost Village

CHARLTON was a small community swept away by extensions to the Filton runway in the late 1940s. As the years pass, folk memories of its size perhaps become exaggerated, but it was certainly large enough to run to a pub, a post office, a chapel, a number of cottages and several imposing houses. The pictures on this page show the Common, a village green complete with ponds. The two large houses in the upper picture were Elmhurst and Gable House Farm.

THE CARPENTER'S ARMS in the 1920s, with members of the Wilmott family on the forecourt.

NEXT TO THE CARPENTER'S ARMS WAS THE POST OFFICE, seen here in the mid 1940s, kept by Mrs Goodfield.

THE COTTAGES, Charlton. On the right is the wife of Harry Bees, the village's harness-maker.

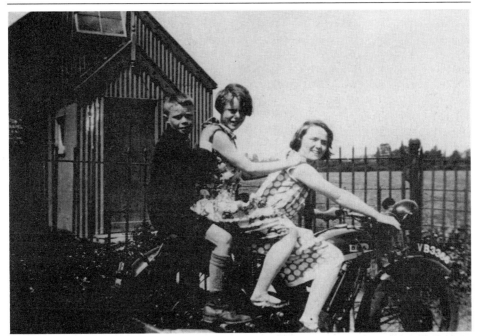

YOUNGSTERS HAVE FUN ON A BSA MOTORBIKE outside the Baptist Church at Charlton. One of the tin huts that has served the Nonconformist movement so well over the years, it previously stood at Littleton-on-Severn.

THE CHARLTON ANNUAL OUTING OF 1920, Weston-bound from outside the Baptist Chapel.

ABOVE: CHARLTON NURSERY IN CATBRAIN LANE, with the type of Edwardian conservatory so fashionable today; and below, also in Catbrain Lane, council houses built shortly after the First World War.

TWO FINE HOUSES LOST THROUGH THE RUNWAY EXTENSIONS. Above: Charlton Farm, with its last owner, Edwin Pierce. In Victorian times it was the home of Christopher Thomas, a leading Bristol soap manufacturer. Below: Gable House Farm is seen in 1888, with members of the Hillier family and assorted vehicles and livestock.

ANOTHER OF THE VILLAGE'S MAJOR HOUSES WAS CHARLTON HOUSE, more usually known as Sunderland's, seen here shortly before demolition.

ON THE FRINGE OF CHARLTON was Pen Park House, which was not in the line of the runway but became derelict, and, like Over Court at Almondsbury, fell prey to vandals' fire. The lodge seen here survives, however, as part of a modern house in Charlton Mead Drive.

Aust, the Ferry and the Severn Bridge

AUST AND THE POST OFFICE IN THE 1920s, when the shop was in the hands of the Kingscott family.

AUST SCHOOL AND PARISH CHURCH. The little school building, now redundant, stands at the entrance to the village beside the busy dual carriageway leading south to Avonmouth from the M4.

THE ROAD TO OLD PASSAGE, Aust, c. 1918, showing the old pier before the ferry opened in 1926.

STORM DAMAGE AT AUST PIER, November 1945, and the *Severn King* discharges pedestrians and cyclists onto a Bailey bridge built by the army.

THE *SEVERN KING* stranded at Aust in 1957. Already talk of the Severn Bridge was rife, and suddenly the ferry, prey to minor disasters such as this, seemed woefully inadequate. Surely that huge structure soon to rise from the depths of the estuary would offer a trouble-free future. . ..

THE QUEUE FOR THE AUST FERRY, August Bank Holiday, 1950.

THE *SEVERN KING* unloading at Aust, early 1960s, with a deck section of the Severn Bridge being lifted into place from the water. The sections were built at Chepstow and floated out into position beneath the bridge on rafts. Below: the bridge is complete, with only the cranes atop the towers breaking up the familiar lines we know today.

A SHADOW OVER THE FERRY — a wonderfully atmospheric picture from that brief period when the little boats and the near-completed bridge coexisted incongruously side by side.

THE *SEVERN KING'S* LAST CROSSING, September 8 1966. The decks were packed for this sentimental journey, with many more left on the jetty.

THEIR WORK ON THE RIVER COMPLETED, the redundant *Severn Queen*, *Severn King* and *Severn Princess* lie at berth in a tucked-away corner of Bristol Docks. Their fate was not so forlorn as it appears; the old workhorses were refurbished and transferred across the Irish Sea to the River Shannon.

ABOVE: THE SEVERN BRIDGE in July 1964, before the painstaking task of raising the deck sections. A dwarfed ferry boat can be seen at Beachley, to the right. Below: just six months later, the deck begins to take shape, working from the centre out to the banks.

THE VIEW FROM THE WELSH TOWER, late 1965, with the Wye bridge nearing completion and the platform sections of the main structure still clearly visible.

A WORLD AWAY from the orchards and smallholdings of days gone by. . . The Aust motorway service area from the English tower, with the cutting up to the toll booths reminding us of the engineering feats involved in even the peripheral work. The bridge has a main span of 3,240 feet suspended from towers 400 feet high, and when it was built it won almost universal acclaim for its lightness and grace. 'Almost as far ahead of its forebears as the jet is in advance of the piston engine,' was one impartial expert's view in 1966. Today, with vastly increased traffic loads and the need for expensive repair work in recent years, it seems only a matter of time before approval is given for a second crossing.

New Passage and Severn Beach

COLLINS'S TEA GARDENS at New Passage was where most trippers in their brakes ended up in Edwardian times, after a brisk constitutional along the front.

New Passage Hotel.

THE SPLENDID NEW PASSAGE HOTEL, built when the Great Western Railway laid a branch out to an ill-fated ferry to Wales, was not always the scene of Victorian decorum. It soon became clear to the railway company that the only way across the river was under it, and from 1874 to 1886 thousands of men burrowed in appalling conditions to construct the 4½-mile Severn Tunnel. On Saturday nights, not unnaturally, they headed for the New Passage for refreshment and conversation with large numbers of young ladies from Bristol who had apparently developed a keen interest in civil engineering; occasionally discussions became heated. The hotel survived until comparatively recent times, but it has now made way for modern housing.

Tea Gardens Entrance, New Passage.

WELCOME TO NEW PASSAGE. Collins's Tea Gardens were the first attraction you came to. In truth, there wasn't too much else. . .

Pumping Station, New Passage.

. . .Unless your taste was for pumping stations. Pumps on either side of the river extract thousands of gallons of springwater every day from the Severn Tunnel, which lies some 50 feet below the estuary. Compact modern pumps spelled the end of the tower that blotted the landscape between New Passage and Severn Beach, but the job goes on just the same. Note the Punch and Judy man on the left of the picture.

NEW PASSAGE BEACH IN ITS HEYDAY. The message from May to Gertie in Weston-super-Mare on the back of the postcard below, dated August 1917, reads: 'Just a card of the glorious beach. Excuse scribble as I am on the pebbles'.

THE ENGLISH PORTAL OF THE SEVERN TUNNEL in the age of steam and below, the approach to the station at Pilning, near by.

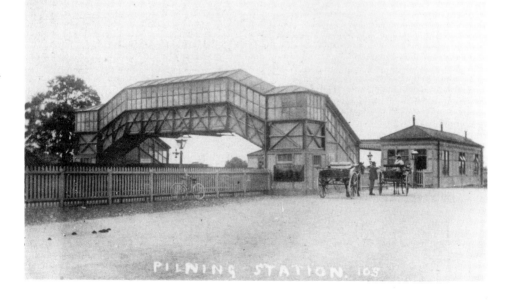

MUCH OF PILNING grew up out of the marshland of the Severn estuary when the tunnel was dug, with a huge influx of construction workers and their families, Welsh and Cornish miners among them. This was the village in around 1910, at the junction of Northwick Road. The pub is the Cross Hands, now greatly altered, and the shop is today's post office.

THE MOTORS POUR INTO SEVERN BEACH — and below, although it's a cold, dull day, it's not long before the trippers are out taking in the sights.

ABOVE: MR BOB STRIDE, the entrepreneur who put Severn Beach on the map, in his later years – and below, the kind of newspaper picture that helped to keep his little resort in the public eye through the 1920s and '30s.

PUTTING and jostling your way to the tea bars and amusement arcades... just two of the delights of Severn Beach in its heyday.

THE PLEASURE GARDENS, they called them. At least if it was cold enough you could always find a bit of comparative peace on the pebbly beach.

HIGHSPOT OF SEVERN BEACH was the huge Blue Lagoon. If you wanted childish fun there were seesaws at the kiddies' end, and if you wanted to look like Esther Williams you sat atop the art deco fountain. . .

...But if the macho image was what you were after, the diving board was the only place to be. It didn't matter, of course, if you never actually got around to diving.

The Amusement Park

ALL THE FUN OF THE FAIR — and below, the joys of one of the quieter children's paddling pools.

CHILDREN'S PADDLING POOL, SEVERN BEACH

IF THE ATTRACTIONS OF THE REFRESHMENT ROOMS PALLED, there was always the option of a picnic on the beach.

ABOVE: A DECKCHAIR NEAR THE ROUNDABOUT was not quite so select as a sojourn in the Rustic
Tea Gardens, below. A residential trailer site of the same name occupies the spot today, one
of the few remaining links with the Severn Beach of the inter-war years.

ABOVE: A REMINDER THAT CHILDREN'S FANCY DRESS PARADES IN 1933 were not so very different from today's, with a Welsh lady, wedding cake, pearly king, sailor, Japanese lady and Red Indian. Little Miss Muffet, on the right, looks as if the spider scared her so much that she spilled her curds and whey all down her dress. Below, the Pavilion Cafe, where perfect days like this often ended with a hot cocoa or Horlicks.

WHAT THE WELL-DRESSED YOUNG LADY TRIPPER WORE to Severn Beach in 1933. The splendid pyjama suits are the kind of garb one associates with the stars of the lavish Busby Berkeley musicals of the day, Ruby Keeler, Ginger Rogers, Joan Blondell *et al*. But obviously just as outré is the swimsuit third from the left – in two colours, no less.

HEALTH AND BEAUTY was no doubt the kind of caption attributed to this newspaper picture of a horsey bathing party in the 1930s. The girls certainly seem to be having fun.

UNHAPPILY, NOT ALL HAS BEEN BEAMING SMILES AND BEACH PARTIES at Severn Beach since then. This was the scene in 1957, when storms breached the sea defences not for the first or last time.

A MORE RECENT TIDAL MISHAP, New Year, 1976, with police and firemen ankle-deep in gardens in Beach Road. Much has been done along the foreshore since then to protect the community from flooding.

ANOTHER MELANCHOLY SCENE. Northavon District Council workmen perform the last rites on the Blue Lagoon prior to landscaping in October, 1980.

BUT THE PICTURES OPPOSITE ARE NO WAY TO LEAVE SEVERN BEACH. Let's return to the bathing belles of 1933, spot the winner, and then turn the page...

DID YOU PICK THE RIGHT GIRL? The husky hunks certainly feel the judges made the correct choice as she is congratulated by Mr Bob Stride.

ACKNOWLEDGEMENTS

Thanks for the loan of pictures, background information or other help are due to:

Mr Arthur Ball • The Revd John Barff • Bristol United Press • British Aerospace
Mr J. Durnell • Mr Edwin and Mrs Carole Ford • Gloucestershire and Avon Life
Mrs Emily Grove • Mr Keith Hardwidge • Mr W. Leslie Harris • Miss Claire Hudson
Mr Christopher Jordan • Mrs Barbara Lansdown • Mr Bert Moss • Mr Don Parker
Mr Colin Powney • Mr H.B. Priestley • Mrs Betty Rickards • Mrs Mary Riddle
Mr Peter Rushby • The Revd Norman Spencer • Mr John St Quinton
Mrs Ethel Thomas • Mr Michael J. Tozer • Miss Mary Trevelyan
Mrs Valerie Vizard • Mr A.D. Walsham • Mrs Julie Walton-Jones